THE
Prayer
MATRIX

LifeChange Books

DAVID JEREMIAH

D0003162

Multnomah® Publishers *Sisters, Oregon*

THE PRAYER MATRIX
published by Multnomah Publishers, Inc.

© 2004 by David P. Jeremiah, Trustee of the David P. Jeremiah Family Trust dated March 15, 1999
Published in association with the literary agency of
Yates and Yates, 1100 Town & Country Rd., Suite 1300, Orange, CA 92868
International Standard Book Number: 1-59052-181-1

Cover image by David Muir/Masterfile

Unless otherwise indicated, Scripture quotations are from:
The Holy Bible, New King James Version © 1984 by Thomas Nelson, Inc.
Other Scripture quotations are from:
The Holy Bible, New International Version (NIV) © 1973, 1984 by International Bible Society,
used by permission of Zondervan Publishing House

The poem on page 20 is adapted from "The Difference" by Grace L. Naessens.

Multnomah is a trademark of Multnomah Publishers, Inc., and is registered in the U.S. Patent and
Trademark Office. The colophon is a trademark of Multnomah Publishers, Inc.

Printed in the United States of America

ALL RIGHTS RESERVED
No part of this publication may be reproduced, stored in a retrieval system, or transmitted,
in any form or by any means—electronic, mechanical, photocopying,
recording, or otherwise—without prior written permission.

For information:
MULTNOMAH PUBLISHERS, INC. • P. O. BOX 1720 • SISTERS, OR 97759

Library of Congress Cataloging-in-Publication Data

Jeremiah, David.
  The prayer matrix / by David Jeremiah.
      p. cm.
  ISBN 1-59052-181-1 (hard)
  1. Prayer. I. Title.
  BV210.3.J47 2004
  248.3'2—dc22

                                              2003022663

04 05 06 07 08 09 10—10 9 8 7 6 5 4 3 2

Contents

OUR GREATEST
GIFT

What's the most wonderful gift in God's great big bag of blessings for us here on earth?

For me, I've found that greatest blessing to be prayer. I believe each of us has a tremendous potential for God through the ministry of praying. It's something attainable by all of us as believers, no matter who we are or what our life circumstances. I'm speaking of something wonderful and joyous and indescribable. It's something God designed to bless us beyond all imagining. And yet it is easily within our reach as a thrilling, daily adventure.

But I must confess to you that prayer can be the hardest work I do, and I suspect there are times when you feel the same way. Even the disciples who lived and walked with Jesus must have had many of the same frustrations with prayer you and I have. Why else would they have come to their Master one day and asked, "Lord, please show us how to pray"?

WHY THE STRUGGLE?

Why is prayer so often difficult? And why does consistent prayer take such discipline on our part?

When I began a battle against cancer a few years ago, I learned something about prayer, and I know of no better way to say it than this: There's prayer, and then there's *prayer*. When things are going smoothly in your life, you pray one way; when you get into a tight spot, you pray another way. Your pleas become more intense; you find yourself crying out to God.

I believe God wants us to pray earnestly like that all the time, on both good days and bad. However, that kind of prayer just doesn't come naturally to us on a regular basis. That's where the discipline comes in—and that's why it's so good for us to be reminded about the value of prayer. My hope in this book is that I might be able to encourage you in some small measure by passing along to you what I have learned along those lines.

TO GREATER DEPTHS

This book is a direct result of my experiences over the past several years. God has taught me more than I can express about personal, particular, persistent praying.

I know that He has been in control of the circumstances that have kept drawing me back to Him in a deeper way. More than ever I know that I need Him, that I'm a child in my relationship to Him, and that He's my Father. I know I think of God more than I did before cancer entered my life. I know I've become more sensitive to His will and to being holy. And I know I've discovered a dimension to prayer that I hadn't realized was even there.

I've discovered a dimension to prayer I hadn't realized was even there.

But I don't write this book as an expert on prayer; I'm nothing but a fellow learner. In fact, I feel like such an infant when it comes to this holy discipline, and I praise and thank the Lord for His patience with me.

It's my profound hope that this book might serve as a springboard to launch even a few of God's people into greater depths of prayer. I've prayed that many who read it will catch the same spirit of excitement that I feel about this subject— because I'm convinced that until we get serious about prayer, we won't know the half of our Lord's desire for our lives.

Chapter 1

FOR THE ASKING

Once when my wife and I were traveling and had gone out to dinner with some friends, my cell phone rang in the middle of our meal. I answered it, and it was our grandson, David Todd, who was four years old at the time.

"Poppy," he said, "where are you?"

I told him where we were.

"Poppy," he said, "could you bring home the shopping mall magazine from the airplane?"

Now that wasn't exactly a request I might have anticipated. But it happened to be a major concern at the time to David Todd.

I found out later (when his dad got on the phone) that on a long airplane flight home with his mother, my grandson had discovered that little magazine in the seat pocket of the airplane that shows pictures of all those wonderful and interesting products. (I think he's inherited some shopping genes from his grandmother.) He started paging through the magazine and looking at all those things, and then got excited to learn that when the flight was over he could actually take the magazine home with him.

However, he went to sleep during the flight, and when the plane landed and they got off, he forgot the magazine. When he remembered it too late, he was quite disappointed.

He had asked me, and that's all he had to do.

❧

So I promised my grandson that I would bring him a copy of that magazine on our way home. He had asked me for it, and that's all he had to do. Why? Because he's my grandson, and anything he requests from me—if it's within my power, and it isn't harmful for him—I'm going to do for him.

I've learned in recent years that that's exactly how God is in His view toward us as we make our requests to Him. But this wasn't the perspective I always held on the matter.

BREAKING DOWN GOD'S RELUCTANCE?

Before I first entered the hospital years ago for cancer treatment, I had the idea in the back of my mind that prayer was breaking down God's reluctance to do something for us. Maybe it was just my previous lack of attention to the Word of God or to those who taught it, but for some reason, this was my underlying attitude about it.

I don't mean that this thought was always consciously in mind whenever I prayed. Nor am I saying I no longer believe we should practice importunity and perseverance in how we pray.

But I've modified my thinking a little about all this, and what I've learned has changed my life. I've discovered that God is in no way dragging His feet about providing what we need. He isn't in heaven calculating whether we've done everything perfectly right so He can in turn do something good for us. Instead, He's waiting and more than willing to provide everything we require.

As He watches over you and me, I don't think He's sitting up in heaven thinking, *If they'll just ask enough times, I'll grant their request.* I think rather that He's in heaven wondering primarily why we don't ask more often.

So where did we get that idea that prayer is breaking down God's reluctance? Why do we tend to think we have to bash in the door of God's unwillingness?

The Bible doesn't teach that view. In fact, the Bible teaches just the opposite about God: He "gives to all liberally and without reproach" (James 1:5). When we're in need, it isn't because of God's reluctance to meet those needs, but because of our reluctance to ask: "You do not have because you do not ask" (James 4:2).

> *We think we have to bash in the door of God's unwillingness.*
>
> ❦

If we ask God for something that's good, and God sees that it's good for us, He'll give it to us, and we'll be able to joyfully affirm with James, "Every good gift and every perfect gift is from above, and comes down from the Father of lights" (James 1:17).

Yet we often don't receive these good and perfect gifts that God so keenly wants to give us, because we simply don't ask for them.

AN OPEN DOOR

There's a God in heaven who loves me more than I can ever know, and who's just waiting for me to come to Him with the needs and requests that are on my heart. And I'm especially reminded of that whenever I read the wonderful words Jesus said about prayer in Matthew 7.

They come near the end of His Sermon on the Mount. Remember what Jesus said there about asking and seeking and knocking?

> "Ask, and it will be given to you; seek, and you will find; knock, and it will be opened to you. For everyone who asks receives, and he who seeks finds, and to him who knocks it will be opened.
> "Or what man is there among you who, if his son asks for bread, will give him a stone? Or if he asks for a fish, will he give him a serpent? If you then, being evil, know how to give good gifts to your children, how much more will your Father who is in heaven give good things to those who ask Him!"

MATTHEW 7:7–11

You've more than likely read those words before. But how fully and completely has it dawned upon you that almighty God, as your loving Father, is eagerly waiting to give you anything and everything you need and request? He has given us, in essence, an open door into His almighty presence and into His infinite storehouse of riches and blessings—for He "is able to do exceedingly abundantly above all that we ask" (Ephesians 3:20).

ENTICEMENT

In this passage in Matthew, these three little words *ask* and *seek* and *knock* are all imperatives. They're commands from the Lord Jesus. He didn't say, "If you feel like asking, then ask." He didn't say, "If you get around to it, why don't you seek?" Or, "If you're in the mood, you may want to try knocking." No, Jesus was telling us, "This is My command to you: Ask, seek, and knock. If you want Me to act on your behalf, then that's how it works. My requirement is that you simply *ask.*" Whatever we need, we must ask for it. And when we don't, we're disobedient to Jesus.

Jesus wants to entice us into praying.

You may sometimes think, I probably shouldn't be wasting God's time by telling Him about my little problems. Or, I don't feel I have any right to ask Him, knowing what kind of person I am, and knowing who God is. But the fact is, the Lord has commanded you to ask Him. Whatever your problems, whatever your needs, whatever difficulties you're experiencing, if you haven't asked God about them, you're disobedient.

But it's also much more than a matter of obedience or disobedience. Our Father in heaven *wants* to hear You express to Him all the things that you feel you truly want and need.

As I read the words of Jesus in that passage, I can't sniff even a particle of guilt anywhere in it (unlike some of the books I've read on prayer, those that seem to be little more than guilt-ridden tirades on why we don't pray and why we should pray more). Jesus doesn't want to goad us into praying as much as He desires to entice us into it.

It's almost as if He says, "Come, partake of My banquet. It's free! Do you see the freshly baked bread piled high on one table? It's for you. Can you smell the delicious aroma of the roasted main course, the sweet fragrance of the pastries and pies and cakes, the wholesome fragrance of newly picked vegetables and fruits? It's all yours! I've provided all you need. I have enough for everyone, and there's no need to fear I'll run out of anything. I'm inviting you to My feast—your place at My table is reserved. All I require is that you *ask* My Father to give you what you need. That's it! That's the only thing lacking."

KEEP ON

Those three little words in Matthew 7:7 are not only imperatives, but in their original Greek tense they have a kind of continuing action connected with them. Jesus is saying *keep on* asking, *keep on* seeking, and *keep on* knocking. Don't ever stop; just keep doing it. Always, whatever you need—just ask.

We could learn a lot from children on that score, couldn't we? I remember hearing a story about a little boy who was at home with his father while the mother was away for the evening. The father (who wasn't as familiar with the boy's bedtime routine as the mother was) was trying to get the boy to sleep. Shortly after tucking his son into bed for the night, he was reading his newspaper when he heard a little voice calling out from the bedroom: "Daddy? I need a drink of water."

The father went upstairs and brought him a drink of water, and of course a short time later the boy called out to say he had to go to the bathroom. Repeatedly the boy kept calling his father to come up and take care of this or that—locating a lost teddy bear, turning on a night light, shutting a closet door.

Finally the exasperated dad reached the limit of his patience. "No more. Young man, you're fine, so get quiet! If I hear another sound from you, I'll come up and give you a spanking!"

For several moments, all was silent. Then the little voice drifted downstairs once more: "Daddy, when you come up here to spank me, could you bring me another drink of water?"

That's how children are. They never quit. It doesn't

matter how many times you say no, they keep coming back. They keep asking. They ask and ask and ask.

A, S, K

These commands in Matthew 7:7 come in a certain kind of progression, with each one a little more intense than the one preceding it. *Ask* is strong enough, but *seek* is stronger, and *knock* is even more intense. Sometimes God wants us to turn up the heat in our prayers for something we're asking from Him.

> *Children never quit. They keep coming back. They ask and ask and ask.*

But the basic thrust of the passage is simply that we're to *ask*. And just so we don't miss its importance, Jesus uses that little word a total of five times in this brief passage on prayer.

In case you're ever explaining this passage to your children or someone else, and they don't seem to be grasping the main point of what Jesus is saying, tell them you'll show it to them in a special code. Have them write down those three basic commands in Matthew 7:7 in a list:

A s k
S e e k
K n o c k

Then take a closer look at the first letters of each word in the list. And there you have it! Simple as that: Just *ask!*

FIRST RESORT

People often come to me, as a pastor, and ask for my advice on some opportunity or decision or difficulty they're facing. Sometimes I'll say, "Have you asked God about it?" And more often than not the reply will be, "Well…no, I guess I haven't."

Let me tell you, asking God about it is always the best place to start, no matter what issue or opportunity you're facing. He needs to be our first resort, not our last. Why would anyone come to David Jeremiah before they approach the Creator of the universe? God has entire worlds in His back pocket; what do I have in comparison to that?

"We pray when there's nothing else we can do," writes Oswald Chambers in *Prayer: A Holy Occupation,* "but Jesus wants us to pray before we do anything at all."

So ask your Father in heaven for whatever it is you need. Ask for provision of your daily necessities. Ask for protection when you're threatened or afraid. Ask Him to show you the right priorities in how you spend your time and money and energy. Ask Him for special guidance when your circumstances call for it.

Make sure you've learned the lesson Grace L. Naessens
learned:

I woke up one morning
    and rushed into the day.
So much to accomplish!
    No time to pray!

Problems tumbled in;
    heavier came each task.
Why doesn't God help me?
    He answered, "You didn't ask."

I wanted joy and beauty
    but all was gray and bleak.
Why doesn't God cheer me?
    He answered, "You didn't seek."

So I approached His door,
    trying all my keys in the lock.
And God lovingly chided me:
    "My child, You didn't knock."

I woke up this morning,
    and thought about the day.
So much to accomplish!
    So I took time to pray.

Chapter 2

ABUNDANT
ANSWERS

Several years ago when I preached about prayer in Matthew 7, our church's superbly creative drama team came up with a great way to set our minds on what Jesus is saying in that passage.

Here's what we saw and heard that Sunday:

On the stage is a sort of vestibule outlined with filing cabinets. A couple is entering the vestibule, and a man is waiting there for them. From their conversation, we learn that this is the threshold of heaven, and the apostle Peter himself is inviting the couple in.

After a brief discussion, the man asks Peter, "What are all these filing cabinets for?"

Peter explains that inside the filing drawers are inventories of all the unclaimed gifts God was prepared to give His children, yet they failed to request them from Him. "One of these cabinets has a drawer marked for you," Peter says. "And in it are all the things God wanted to give you that you never asked for."

I'll never forget that! If there were a drawer like that in heaven for you and me, how full would it be? Some of us may be shocked in eternity to realize the potential ministry impact we could have had, and the true blessings we could have known, if we'd only just asked God for them.

UNCONDITIONAL PROMISES

After telling us to ask and seek and knock, Jesus goes on in Matthew 7:8 to make some unconditional promises. Notice what He says:

"Everyone who asks…" What's the next word? *Receives.*

"He who seeks…" What's next? *Finds.*

"And to him who knocks, it will be…" Will be what? *Opened.*

Do you see any loopholes in those promises? Does He say there anywhere that God answers some prayers but not others? Does that passage imply that if we pray, God might hear us, or He might not?

No, God's guarantee for us is this: He hears and

answers *every* prayer. Ask and receive, seek and find, knock and watch the door open—these are ironclad promises. Now I know that there are other passages in Scripture that teach further guidelines for prayer—things like praying according to God's will, praying in Jesus' name, and praying in the Spirit. But the fact is, in this passage, Jesus strongly teaches the profound effectiveness of simply asking, without weighing the process down with any restrictions.

In his profound book *With Christ in the School of Prayer,* Andrew Murray says it simply and powerfully: "God means prayer to have an answer." And we see plenty of evidence for that in the pages of God's Word.

> *Prayer has paved the way for the conversion of millions of people.*

Prayer opened the Red Sea.

Prayer brought water from the rock and bread from heaven.

Prayer made the sun stand still.

Prayer brought fire from the sky on Elijah's sacrifice.

Prayer overthrew armies and healed the sick.

Prayer raised the dead.

The same has always been true, down through all the centuries that have followed Bible times. Prayer has paved the way for the conversion of millions of people. Things that we think are impossible, God does when people pray.

SMALL PRAYERS TOO

And He not only answers big prayers; the little ones get answered too.

I remember a wonderful story about a woman whose young daughter was taken ill one morning at school. After the mother received a call from the school, she picked up her little girl, took her home, and called the doctor and described her daughter's symptoms. The doctor reported that there seemed to be quite an outbreak of this flulike affliction, and because of the number of people coming in to be treated for it, he wouldn't be able to see the girl until later in the afternoon. For the meantime, he suggested an over-the-counter medicine that the mother could pick up to help her daughter.

The mother put her daughter to bed and tucked her in, then told her she was going to the store for the medicine. "I'll be back in just a few minutes," she said.

She rushed to the store and purchased the medicine, but when she returned to the parking lot, she discovered she'd left her keys in the car. Looking through the window, she could see them dangling from the ignition. And the car was locked.

The first response that came to her mind was to use her cell phone and call her daughter to explain that she was going to be delayed. When she did, her daughter told her, "Mommy, get a coat hanger. I've seen on television how they just stick a coat hanger down the window to unlock the door."

The mother went back inside the store and was able to get a wire coat hanger, though she had her doubts about whether it would work. In fact, she felt embarrassed, because she wasn't sure at all how to use the coat hanger to open her car door. But she was a woman of prayer, so as she left the store she lifted up her heart to the heavenly

"I don't know what to do, Lord."

Father: "I don't know what to do, Lord. My keys are locked in the car, and my little girl is home sick. I've got this coat hanger here, but I don't know what to do with it. Please send somebody to help me."

As she finished her prayer, a car immediately pulled up at the curb right where she was standing and dropped off a passenger. The man who got out must be God's answer, the woman concluded, though he didn't seem like the kind of package God would send—he had a rough look and hadn't shaved for some time, and she thought he might be a homeless person. But she said to him, "Sir, can you help me?"

"What's the problem?" he said.

"I locked my keys in the car, and I've got this coat hanger, but I don't know what to do with it."

"Lady," he said, "where's your car?"

Why does God answer any of our prayers?

❧

She took him to it, and after bending the coat hanger and inserting it over the top of the window, he quickly got the door open.

The mother was so overwhelmed that she put her arms around this scruffy guy and gave him a hug to thank him. "You're such a good man," she told him.

"Lady," he replied, "I'm no good man. I just got out of prison."

As the man walked away, the mother prayed, "Thank You, Lord! You sent me a professional!"

WHY GOD ANSWERS

Why did God answer this woman's prayer in such a pointed way for her? Why does He answer any of our prayers?

Oswald Chambers, in his typically pointed style, wrote this in his book *If You Will Ask*:

There is only one kind of person who can really pray, and that is the child-like saint, the simple, stupid, supernatural child of God; I do mean "stupid."

Well, I don't know about you, but I guess that means I qualify as someone who can pray! Chambers then goes on to say that it's "nonsense" to try and use mental reasoning to explain why God answers those "stupid" prayers. "God answers prayer," he writes, "on the ground of redemption and on no other ground. Let us never forget that our prayers are heard, not because we are in earnest, not because we suffer, but because Jesus suffered."

His point about redemption gets a lot of support from the book of Hebrews, where we're reminded that it's "by the blood of Jesus" that we have "boldness" to enter God's presence with our prayers (Hebrews 10:19). The mystery of why God answers prayer is all wrapped up in the mystery of why He redeemed us; just like the Cross, it points to an infinite love that is far beyond any human explanation.

REMEMBERING WHAT GOD DOES

Since I started keeping a journal years ago and writing down my requests, it has been thrilling for me to look back to see what God has done in my life in response to my prayers. Again and again I see how God will eventually answer requests that I had almost forgotten about. Sometimes the answers are so specific that it's almost frightening. To think that God, the Ruler of the universe, would do that for me for no other reason than that I asked! It staggers me.

> *Sometimes the answers are so specific it's almost frightening.*

Seeing repeated answers has got to be one of the most powerful motivators to continued prayer. If you're like me, it's easy to overlook or forget what God has done for you.

One year as I approached yet another birthday, I was feeling very low. Then one day I received a birthday card from a friend and a member of our church. He did more than wish me a happy birthday; he included a note that recounted for me some of the blessings I'd experienced since my last birthday:

Healed from a terrible disease, sold a house and built a new one (no mean feat in these challenging times), had a son do remarkably well on the football field and win a county championship, had a daughter get married, had a radio program grow to major proportions, got a son and daughter-in-law back to California and into a new home, preached wonderful sermons each Sunday several times to a huge number of people, led a vibrant school system (preschool through college), managed a complex system of ministries (from in-home Bible studies to missionaries throughout the world)…and the list goes on and on. And this from the perspective of one who just sees a small part of what is happening from a seat in the congregation.

Reading that pulled me out of the doldrums. I knew that all of those things on that long list had been items for prayer in the previous year. I could only thank the Lord for allowing me another year of life on earth and for being so gracious and helpful to me in all that He had accomplished in my life.

ASKING AND GETTING

R. A. Torrey has written some of the best books on prayer ever published, but there was a time when his prayer life couldn't get off the ground. Then a day came, Torrey writes, "when I realized what real prayer meant, realized that prayer was having an audience with God, actually coming into the presence of God, and asking and getting things from Him."

That realization transformed his prayer life:

Before that, prayer had been a mere duty, and sometimes a very irksome duty, but from that time on prayer has been not merely a duty, but a privilege, one of the most highly esteemed privileges of life.

Before that the thought that I had was, "How much time must I spend in prayer?" The thought that now possesses me is, "How much time may I spend in prayer without neglecting the other privileges and duties of life?"

As you get a deeper and deeper picture of how prayer means being in the presence of God to both ask for and receive His blessings, I hope that you, too, will begin to find it one of the highest privileges in your life.

Chapter 3

SO MUCH MORE

As I look back, some of God's answers to prayer in my life stand out to me in particularly large letters.

Here's just one of them:

My son Daniel was quarterback of his high school football team and set a number of passing records. One day, when he was still a junior, he asked me, "Dad, if I continue to be able to play well, and if I'm offered a scholarship, and it's a secular school and not a Christian school, will you let me go?"

I didn't think about it a whole lot. I said, "Son, go anyplace you want, and I know you'll be okay."

Well that was good for his junior year. When he got to be a senior, he was still playing outstandingly well, and the recruiters were calling, and he was trying to figure out what to do. I began to wonder if I'd given him the right answer to that question the previous year.

Through a complex series of events and connections, Daniel decided to enroll as a freshman with a football scholarship at Northeast Louisiana University in Monroe, Louisiana. When I knew this was the direction Daniel was headed, I tried to find out more about what was going on there and what kind of place it was. I couldn't recall having ever met a Christian from Louisiana, and I'd heard things about Mardi Gras and so on, so I began to get worried.

SOMEONE TO HELP

If you looked in my journal at the things I wrote in those months before Daniel went off to college, you would see, day after day, my prayers for God to help me locate some-body in Monroe, Louisiana, who was a believer, someone whom Daniel could have connections with, someone who could help him in his life as a student. I prayed that prayer for months.

One day I was in my office and the phone rang. I picked it up, and the voice on the other end had the most wonderful Southern accent I'd ever heard. The caller intro-duced himself as Richard Giannini, the athletic director at Northeast Louisiana. He said he'd recently been playing golf "with a preacher friend" who'd asked him about the latest new recruits for the football team. "I told him we just signed a boy from California named Daniel Jeremiah."

With his interest perked, the golfing partner had asked, "What does his father do?"

"I think he's a preacher," the athletic director answered. His partner then mentioned that he knew about me and my ministry.

"So, I'm sitting here in my office this morning," Mr. Giannini continued telling me, "and I'm thinking, I bet that man back in California wonders if there's anybody out here for his son who's a Christian. And I just wanted to call you and let you know that I'm a believer. I just got back from Promise Keepers. I'm in a couple of accountability groups here in Monroe, and I go to the First Baptist Church, and you tell that boy of yours that if he needs anything, if he needs somebody to talk with, or if he gets discouraged, he can just knock on my door, and I'll be there for him."

Then he added, "By the way, the president of our university is a believer, too, and his wife listens to you on the radio every day."

After we ended the conversation, I set the phone down and began to cry. I looked back over the pages of my journal and saw how often I'd asked God for somebody there in Louisiana for my son—and now He had given me the school's athletic director and the president!

NOT ALWAYS YES

God always answers prayer, even though sometimes He may not give us the answer we particularly want, or when we want it. He always answers sincere prayer—but His answer isn't always yes.

I remember reading this little paradigm from Bill Hybels some years ago, and I wrote it in the front of my Bible. It goes like this:

If the *request* is wrong, God says, "No."

If *you* are wrong, God says, "Grow."

If the *timing* is wrong, God says, "Slow."

And if the request is right, and you are right, and the timing is right, God says, "Go!"

In that paradigm, the part that's most difficult for me is not the answer "no"; it's the answer "slow." I always want God to answer my prayers *right now.* I want to pray and then feel that when I get up off my knees, God already has the answer at my door.

And God does that for us sometimes, but many times He puts us in a storm, or He waits for a period of time so we can keep praying and can grow our prayer wings and be stronger than we otherwise would be.

God sometimes has to delay the answer to our prayers until we're mature enough to receive it. If you're a fifteen-year-old boy and you pray for a motorcycle, God might answer yes to that prayer, but maybe not right then. He might wait until you're a little older so you don't go out and kill yourself on it.

Answers to prayer have to be on God's schedule, not ours. He hears us pray, and He answers according to His will in His own time. But that shouldn't keep us from praying persistently to Him.

> *Answers to prayer have to be on God's schedule.*

THANKFUL FOR THE NO'S

Will God give us every little thing we want and ask for? No, He hasn't promised to do that. He's promised to give us the things we need, and only for today. God hasn't promised to fulfill our every fantasy. We may pray for a new luxury car, but it may be His will for us to drive a used compact. There's nothing wrong with either vehicle; both can provide the transportation we need. And meeting our needs is what God has promised to do.

I recall reading a statement by Ruth Graham—Billy Graham's wife—who said that if God had given her everything she asked for, she would have married the wrong man seven times.

Maybe you, too, have lived long enough (I know I

have) to be thankful for the fact that God hasn't answered yes to all your prayers. Maybe it was something you deeply wanted and fervently prayed for, but you can see now that it wouldn't have been the best for you, and so there's a spirit of gratitude in your heart that God's answer then was no.

Frequently God has to first change me so He can answer my prayer.

❧

Even when we ask amiss, our prayer can still bring God's will into sharper focus for us. I've found that frequently God has to first change *me* so He can answer my prayer. Sometimes my prayer is misconceived. On occasion I've prayed for something, thinking I knew all the issues when in fact I did not; I wasn't even close! But as I continued to pray, God helped me see that my whole perspective was skewed. He then tweaked my prayers and massaged them and refined them—and then He answered. It's as if He then was telling me, *"That's* the prayer I want you to pray." And I have received my request.

CHANGES

I like to think that every time we pray, we're somehow and in some way changed. That fact in itself should draw us to prayer, if we desire to be like God.

Oswald Chambers (in *If You Will Ask*) even goes so far as to say this:

> It is not so true that "Prayer changes things" as that prayer changes us, and then we change things.... Prayer is not altering things externally, but working wonders within our disposition. When we pray, things remain the same, but we begin to be different.

These are the kinds of changes within that we need to be praying for. In his book *The Possibilities of Prayer*, E. M. Bounds says it's only by prayer that we gain the ability "to feel the law of love, to speak according to the law of love, and to do everything in harmony with the law of love.... We need Divine aid to act brotherly, wisely, and nobly, and to judge truly, and charitably. God's help to do all these things in God's way is secured by prayer."

THE WHY BEHIND THE NO'S

I know some Christians spend little time praying because they have a hard time believing they'll see significant answers. Perhaps they prayed in the past for something of vital interest to them and didn't receive the answer they hoped for. So they've mostly stopped praying.

They easily identify with what J. Oswald Sanders wrote in *Effective Prayer:* "It is easy to become a fatalist in reference to prayer. It is easier to regard unanswered prayer as the will of God than to…reason out the causes of the defeat."

> *God always answers prayer.*

And what could be some of those causes for defeat?

Maybe one cause is that we too easily look at issues from our point of view rather than from God's perspective. On that score, Oswald Chambers gives us a lot to think about:

> Our Lord in His teaching regarding prayer never once referred to unanswered prayer; He said God always answers prayer. If our prayers are in the name of Jesus, that is, in accordance with His nature, the answers will not be in accordance with our nature, but with His. We are apt to forget this, and to say without thinking that God does not always answer prayer. He does every time, and when we are in close communion with Him, we realize that we have not been misled.

But what if you believe you're sincerely praying in God's will for something He delights in, and yet there seems to be no positive answer?

When that's our situation, James Montgomery Boice has a very practical suggestion for us in his commentary *The Sermon on the Mount:*

> If you are praying for something and God is not answering your request with a "Yes," ask what you can accomplish in the meantime and give yourself to that. It does not mean that God may not give you what you are asking for eventually, but in the meantime you will be doing good work.

That's excellent advice!
And the best advice of all is this: Just keep praying!

Chapter 4

THE MATRIX

In your own journey of discovery about prayer, somewhere along the way I'm sure you've wondered the same thing I have:

Why do we have to pray—since God already knows what we need?

And God does, of course, know all our needs; Jesus Himself says so. He mentions that fact twice in the Sermon on the Mount, before telling us to ask and seek and knock: "Your Father knows the things you have need of before you ask Him" (Matthew 6:8); "For your heavenly Father knows that you need all these things" (6:32).

God obviously knows our condition and our true needs and even our desires far better than we ever will. So why does He tell us to bring our requests before Him?

There are several reasons, I think. I've discovered, for example, that when I'm able to tell God about a need I'm sensing so deeply in my heart, then no matter how difficult and challenging that need may be, I gain a renewed confidence that God will be at work on my behalf to meet it. At the same time, I begin to understand my own situation in greater detail and with much more clarity—all because I consciously bring that need before Him in prayer.

HARD-WIRED

But the biggest reason for why God asks us to pray—a reason we can't avoid—is this: Scripture insists that God has hard-wired the universe in such a way that He works primarily through prayer. God has set up creation so that the way He does His work is through the prayers of His children. At the moment we pray, we become subject to the most powerful force in the universe.

> *God has hard-wired the universe so that He works primarily through prayer.*

And when we don't pray, we short-circuit what God wants to do. When we fail to pray, we cuff God's hand. I don't mean that in a disrespectful way, because God can do anything He wants. But I know from my study of the Word of God that He has ordained the processes of the world in such a manner that He accomplishes His will through the requests offered up by His people.

When we neglect prayer, we actually limit what God might do in our lives and in the lives of others. You may be a little hesitant to accept the truth of that statement. But if it weren't true, what could James mean when he writes, "Yet you do not have because you do not ask" (James 4:2)?

Or think of Paul: If he didn't believe the prayers of his friends actually had power to change his own circumstances, it would be sheer nonsense for him to write to them the following words:

> Now I beg you, brethren…that you strive together with me in your prayers to God for me.
>
> ROMANS 15:30

> I know that this will turn out for my salvation through your prayer.
>
> PHILIPPIANS 1:19

> Pray also for me, that whenever I open my mouth, words may be given me so that I will fearlessly make known the mystery of the gospel.
>
> EPHESIANS 6:19, NIV

And pray for us…that God may open a door for our message, so that we may proclaim the mystery of Christ…. Pray that I may proclaim it clearly, as I should.

COLOSSIANS 4:3–4, NIV

Finally, brethren, pray for us, that the word of the Lord may have free course and be glorified.

2 THESSALONIANS 3:1

Prepare a guest room for me, for I trust that through your prayers I shall be granted to you.

PHILEMON 1:22
(PAUL WROTE THESE WORDS WHILE STILL IN PRISON.)

Paul and the other apostles knew that God might well withhold certain of His blessings from them if they and their fellow believers neglected to pray. Therefore they prayed, and they recruited others to pray, never wanting to curb what God might be pleased to do.

If we want all the blessing God has available to give us, we too must pray. "It is on prayer," says Andrew Murray, "that the promises wait for their fulfillment, the kingdom for its coming, the glory of God for its full revelation."

That's what *your* prayers can bring into reality!

GETTING THINGS DONE

Let me say it once more: God works in our world primarily through prayer. No doubt He could have selected some other method, but He has chosen to do most of His work through prayer. In certain unexplainable ways, He has made Himself subservient to the prayers of His people.

And therefore, from our perspective, we find that prayer is what gets things done.

I scoured the New Testament some time ago, looking for things God does in ministry that are *not* prompted by prayer. Do you know what I found? Nothing. *Everything* God does in the work of ministry, He does through prayer.

Consider:

- Prayer is the way we defeat the devil (Luke 22:32; James 4:7).
- Prayer is the way we help to save the lost (Luke 18:13).
- Prayer is the way we acquire wisdom (James 1:5).
- Prayer is the way a backslider gets restored (James 5:16–20).
- Prayer is how the saints get strengthened (Jude 1:20, Matthew 26:41).
- Prayer is the way we get laborers out to the mission field (Matthew 9:38).

- Prayer is how we cure the sick (James 5:13–15).
- Prayer is how we accomplish the impossible (Mark 11:23–24).

Everything we do that's worth doing, everything God wants to do in the church, everything God wants to do in your life—all of this He has subjugated to one thing: Prayer.

THE ACTION TRIGGER

The same thing was true in the book of Acts. Acts is like a handbook on prayer. Everywhere you turn, the disciples are praying, and as a result, remarkable things happen. Prayer triggers God's action.

This is true from the very first chapter, where the first believers gathered in an upper room, and "these all continued with one accord in prayer and supplication" (1:14). That was the church's foundation—it all got started through prayer. Then came the Day of Pentecost, when the Holy Spirit came down upon them, and Peter preached, and three thousand new believers were added.

Afterward, all these new Christians "continued steadfastly…in prayers" (2:42). When opposition against them heated up, "they raised their voice to God with one accord" (4:24). God's response was quick and awesome: "And when they had prayed, the place where they were assembled together was shaken; and they were all filled with the Holy Spirit, and they spoke the word of God with boldness" (4:31).

The apostles made prayer a top priority ("We will give ourselves continually to <u>prayer</u>"—6:4). We see the church praying when deacons and elders are selected (6:5–6, 14:23) and when missionaries are sent out (13:3). And we see prayer when they faced emergency needs, such as when Peter was thrown in prison (12:5, 12).

There was no such thing in those early days as a powerful church without prayer…just as in our day there will never be such a thing as a powerful church without prayer. "Well," some may say, "those were New Testament days, and we're beyond that now." But if you trace the life of the church of Jesus Christ from two thousand years ago all the way up to this moment, you will discover that all the great revivals and awakenings of church history were fueled by the power of prayer.

> *There is no such thing as a powerful church without prayer.*

THE MYSTERY OF THE MATRIX

So it is that God has made certain things dependent upon prayer, things that will never be done unless we pray. Could God do whatever He chooses without our prayer? Of course. But God has determined that He will use the prayers of His people to accomplish His purposes of salvation and redemption on this earth, and His purpose of bringing glory to His name for all eternity.

When Jesus tells us in Matthew 7 to ask and to seek and to knock, it wasn't the first time in the Sermon on the Mount that He'd spoken about prayer. Earlier (in Matthew 6:5–8) He taught us not to pray publicly to impress others, and not to pray with "vain repetitions" of words to impress God (He doesn't want mere language from us; He wants real communication). Jesus then went on to give us an outline for prayer's content (Matthew 6:9–13), an outline we commonly call the Lord's Prayer. And in that outline we see more of the mystery of the prayer matrix:

The God who has made it perfectly clear in the pages of the Bible that He's in control of every detail in this universe, and who promises that He will reign as King for all eternity, still asks us to pray, "Your kingdom come. Your will be done on earth as it is in heaven" (Matthew 6:10).

The God who has lovingly promised throughout Scripture to be our faithful Father and Provider still asks us to daily pray, "Give us this day our daily bread" (6:11).

The God who has given us the priceless gift of forgiveness through the death of His Son still asks us to pray, "And forgive us our debts, as we forgive our debtors" (6:12).

The God who is our Good Shepherd, who promises to

lead us in paths of righteousness, who
has pledged to protect us from Satan's
power and to not let us be tempted
beyond what we can bear, still asks us
to pray, "And do not lead us into
temptation, but deliver us from the
evil one" (6:13).

*In obedience to
the spiritual laws
of this universe,
we pray.*

And so in obedience to His commands and to the spiritual laws of
this universe, we pray. And as we pray, the kingdom and the
power and the glory are indeed His forever!

YOUR BEST WORK

"Prayer is everything," Oswald Chambers wrote. Whatever's
happening in this world for God, prayer is always at the
critical center.

Andrew Murray seemed to understand this about as
well as anybody, as evidenced in *With Christ in the School
of Prayer*. He declared this about prayer: "The powers of the
eternal world have been placed at its disposal." He describes
prayer as "the very essence of true religion, the channel of
all blessings, the secret of power and life." Murray looked at
the commands and promises Jesus gave us about prayer in
Matthew 7:7–8 and called them "the fixed eternal law of
the kingdom." And he added, "Though in its beginnings

prayer is so simple that the feeblest child can pray, yet it is at the same time the highest and holiest work to which man can rise."

You can literally affect what is going on throughout this world by praying.

❦

Prayer is the greatest and best thing for God you'll ever do. "Prayer does not fit us for the greater works," writes Oswald Chambers; "prayer *is* the greater work." Murray speaks of prayer as "the highest part of the work entrusted to us, the root and strength of all other work."

You can commit your life to a ministry of prayer, and thereby touch the world. You can go to Africa, to China, to India, to Russia, to the Middle East, to South America—anywhere, by going to the throne of God in prayer for those men and women who serve the kingdom's work out among all of those places. You can literally affect what is going on throughout this world by praying. But you've got to pray.

Listen again to Andrew Murray: "Christ has opened the school of prayer specially to train intercessors for the great work of bringing down, by their faith, and prayer, the blessings of His work and love on the world around."

It ought to take away our breath to realize that our almighty God invites us to have such a huge part in the work of bringing in His kingdom for all eternity.

Chapter 5

THE
INTERCHANGE
OF LOVE

In the early 1960s, Americans were captivated by photos showing President Kennedy's young children playing with their toys on the carpeted floor of the Oval Office. I doubt any other kids were allowed into the office of the president of the United States, but John Jr. and Caroline were. And even though the man behind that desk was the nation's President and the leader of the Free World, those little children playing at his feet just called him Daddy.

That's how it is with us and God. He's the holy, awesome, almighty Sovereign of the universe and Lord of glory, but He's also our Father. In prayer we can come confidently into the presence of such a holy and powerful and majestic God because we're His dearly beloved children.

When my own kids were growing up, it was understood that if they ever came during the week to my church office, they could always get in to see me. It didn't matter when they came or who I was with. When my secretary rang my phone and told me that one of my children wanted to see me, I would excuse myself and greet them. While I couldn't do that with everybody—it would be chaos—I could do it for my son or for my daughter. After all, a special bond exists between us. I'm their father! They can walk into my life any time they choose.

On the cross, Jesus opened up the way for you to be adopted into God's family. That special bond is there, and always will be. Because you've put your faith in Him, you can now go whenever you choose into the presence of God Almighty, and He'll meet with you and hear whatever you have to say.

ALWAYS AT THE FRONT OF THE LINE

That's true for all God's children, not just some.

Remember what Jesus said in Matthew 7:8? "For everyone who asks receives, and he who seeks finds, and to him who knocks it will be opened." In your thinking, let me ask you to underline one little word there—the word *everyone*. Let it jump off the page at you. God's eager willingness to answer your prayers is a comprehensive promise that includes every single Christian.

When it comes to hearing His children, God's ears aren't at all selective. You never fall behind Billy Graham in getting your prayers heard and answered. No one stands in line ahead of you, with you way back in the middle or at the end. You're always at the front. God hears *every* child of His who comes in prayer before his Almighty Father.

No one stands in line ahead of you.

❧

That word *everyone* means everyone, including you and me. God hears your prayers, God hears mine.

You may think, *But I'm not that great a Christian. I haven't done all I know I should do, so I have my doubts whether God would hear me right now.* But if you think that, you're denying the Word of God, because He tells us that everyone who asks will be heard.

THE MATRIX AGAIN

Here's something else for you to think about concerning the "prayer matrix" we looked at earlier: Prayer is built into the way the universe works because the universe works on *relationship*—our personal relationship with God. That defines everything. That's the ultimate reality. And there's nothing that proves our relationship with God more than our prayers.

Think again about that prayer outline Jesus taught us in the Lord's Prayer, and how it demonstrates the importance of relationship:

Our Father in heaven—there's the Father/child relationship, as well as the Superior/subordinate relationship.

Hallowed be Your name—the Deity/worshipper relationship.

Your kingdom come—the Sovereign/subject relationship.

Your will be done—the Master/servant relationship.

Give us this day our daily bread—the Benefactor/beneficiary relationship.

Forgive us our debts—the Savior/sinner relationship.

Do not lead us into temptation—the Guide/pilgrim or Leader/follower relationship.

Deliver us from the evil one—the Guardian/dependent relationship.

For Yours is the kingdom and the power and the glory forever—the Creator/creature relationship.

Every aspect of our rich and many-sided relationship with God is meant to be constantly brought out and expressed through our words of prayer and praise to Him. That's just the way the universe works.

STONES OR BREAD? FISH OR SNAKES?

To help us really grab hold of this relational side to prayer, Jesus in Matthew 7 gave us an interesting illustration after commanding us to ask and seek and knock:

> Or what man is there among you who, if his son asks for bread, will give him a stone? Or if he asks for a fish, will he give him a serpent?
>
> MATTHEW 7:9–10

Many stones in Palestine have a similar shape and color to the small round loaves of bread that were commonly baked in those days. It was a resemblance that was easy for anyone to see—especially if you were hungry. (As when Jesus was fasting in the wilderness, and Satan tempted Him with these words: "If You are the Son of God, command that these stones become bread"— Matthew 4:3.)

When Jesus was preaching about prayer in the Sermon on the Mount, there may well have been many of those round loaflike stones scattered across the ground where the crowd was sitting as they listened. So Jesus asked His listeners to consider whether any parents among them would give a stone to their child if the child asked for bread. The answer was obvious to all: Of course not.

This hillside where Jesus was preaching happened to overlook the Sea of Galilee, where fishermen each day cast their nets, and fish was a common food for all the people listening to Jesus that day. Sometimes as the fishermen drew in their nets, water snakes were mixed in with the catch. Perhaps Jesus had this in mind as He asked His listeners whether any of the parents there would offer a snake if their child asked for fish. Again the obvious answer was no.

GOOD THINGS

Then Jesus sharpened His point:

> If you then, being evil, know how to give good gifts to your children, how much more will your Father who is in heaven give good things to those who ask Him!
>
> MATTHEW 7:11

None of us is anywhere near as good as God—we're terribly flawed, and far from perfect. In fact, in comparison to the purity and infinite love and goodness of God, we're evil. And yet even in our sinfulness we would never think of substituting rocks for bread or snakes for fish when our children ask us for food. (I suppose there are some deranged people who would do such a thing, but none of the parents I know

We want to do the best we can for our kids.

❦

would do it.) We want to do the best we can for our kids; if they ask for something, and it's reasonable, and we think it's good for them, we'll grant their request. That's how we as parents think today, and it's how parents thought back in Jesus' day as well.

Jesus was counting on just such a reaction from His listeners. So He drove home His lesson: How can you imagine that your heavenly Father would want to do anything less for you than human parents want to do for their children? He will indeed do that much for us—and "much more" besides! He gives to those who ask, and He gives "good things"!

This illustration from Jesus was carefully designed to convince us that God longs to answer the prayers of His beloved sons and daughters. And God is waiting for you and me to get in on His willingness to give His children good things. He's waiting for us to pray to our Father so He can act on our behalf.

KNOW HIM BETTER

Why is it that our churches aren't doing better? Why is it that our homes sometimes get so terribly messed up? I believe it's because we don't often enough ask God to help us. And maybe the reason we aren't asking is that we simply fail to pursue our relationship with Him as we should.

"There is a direct correlation between not knowing Jesus well and not asking much from Him," John Piper writes. "A failure in our prayer life is generally a failure to know Jesus."

But it doesn't have to be that way.

"The good of praying," says Oswald Chambers, "is that it gets us to know God." He also reminds us, "The only place to rest is in God, and the only way to come to God is by prayer."

"It is in prayer and its answer that the interchange of love between the Father and His child takes place," Andrew Murray tells us. And he adds: "It is to prayer that God has given the right to take hold of Him and His strength."

Isn't it time that we took hold of more of God, and more of His strength? And the way it happens is with more prayer.

Chapter 6

DECLARATION
OF DEPENDENCE

Years ago, at a time when I needed a break from a hectic schedule, my family took a quick trip up to Lake Arrowhead in the San Bernardino Mountains of Southern California. It was a wonderful, refreshing recovery time. Somehow when you go to the mountains, it helps clear your head, and as I hiked around that weekend, I did a lot of thinking.

I understood, maybe for the first time, why it's so critical to develop a strong and deep relationship with Jesus Christ. I realized there's simply no other relationship on earth that can meet our ultimate needs. That's no fault of ours or anyone else's. It's simply how we were created. We may think it's unfair, but it's just the way life is.

It's a part of that matrix we're discovering.

As I walked around Lake Arrowhead on that occasion, I wrote something down. Here it is: "Jesus Christ, the same yesterday, today, and forever." If we put our hopes and pour our lives into anything else besides Him, it's certain that we'll be ultimately disappointed. But if we put our hopes and pour our lives into Jesus Christ, we'll ultimately find far more fulfillment and blessing than we can ever imagine.

BIG PROBLEMS, BIG SOLUTIONS

Sometimes we can get so overwhelmed and discouraged by the desperate needs and difficulties we experience in our lives. But could it be that one reason we have great problems is that God wants to show us great solutions? He longs to show us the riches of His grace and the poverty of our own resources. Prayer is uniquely designed to demonstrate both truths.

One reason we have great problems is that God wants to show us great solutions.

That's why God encourages us with these words: "Let us therefore come boldly to the throne of grace, that we may obtain mercy and find grace to help in time of need" (Hebrews 4:16).

Prayer and our times of need go hand in hand.

SHUT UP

When I battled cancer, the lesson I learned that struck home with most force was this: *I discovered I was helpless without God.* I learned how to pray out of desperation.

In *Fresh Wind, Fresh Fire,* Jim Cymbala said something I can easily identify with: "Prayer cannot truly be taught by principles and seminars and symposiums. It has to be born out of a whole environment of felt need. If I say, 'I *ought* to pray,' I will soon run out of motivation and quit; the flesh is too strong. I have to be *driven* to pray."

The Scottish preacher Andrew Bonar is credited with making this statement a century and a half ago: "God likes to see His people shut up to this: That there is no hope but in prayer."

At least initially, serious prayer is almost always driven by such desperate necessity. We don't pray because we ought to; we pray because we are without any other recourse. I think God likes to see His people coming to Him in desperation and casting themselves upon His mercy. Only then do we recognize reality for what it is.

KEEP BUZZING THE NURSE

One day I finally recognized with particular clarity why it was so hard for me to pray, and that day I wrote this down in my Bible: "Prayer is my Declaration of Dependence." For a go-getter, type A, driven person like me, prayer is difficult because it flies in the face of our frantic efforts to prove that we're self-sufficient, independent, and strong.

With prayer I have to admit I'm spiritually impotent.

Prayer flies in the face of our frantic efforts to prove we're self-sufficient.

John Piper in *Desiring God* calls prayer "the antidote for the disease of self-confidence." He then goes on to point out a telling difference between Uncle Sam and Jesus Christ: "Uncle Sam won't enlist you in his service unless you are healthy, and Jesus won't enlist you unless you are sick." It's just as Jesus said: "Those who are well have no need of a physician, but those who are sick. I did not come to call the righteous, but sinners, to repentance" (Mark 2:17).

Piper then notes that "Christianity is fundamentally convalescence ('Pray without ceasing' = Keep buzzing the nurse)."

My bout with cancer taught me a lot about "buzzing the nurse"! The fears and desperation which forced me to my knees taught me to cry out to God as never before. And do you know what? God heard! He answered! He delivered me from all my fears. And I know He desires to do the same for you.

IT'S THE TRUTH

We become men and women of prayer when we recognize our desperate need. Our culture teaches that we don't need God because we ourselves are god. Prayer stabs at the heart of that idea. God tells us that we're dependent upon Him, and He doesn't say that just to lord it over us; He's telling the truth, and we can either accept it by faith or have to learn this lesson the hard way through the difficulties of life.

One day I recorded the following in my journal:

> I am writing these prayers to You because my mind so easily wanders from the thought process when I pray in another way. I want to be working things out with You in my prayer time, and I believe that I am learning how to do that, at least in some measure. I realize more than ever before that this time is more important than sermon preparation, or even than the preaching of a sermon. If I do not work things out with You, I am doomed to failure and frustration and fatigue!

I have learned, and am learning, that there's no real victory or joy in the Christian life unless there's also a sense of total dependence upon God. And that sense of dependence is what makes prayer spring to life.

Think about it: When Jesus walked upon this earth as both God and man, He lived as a man in dependence upon His Father, giving us an example of how we're to live. And if Jesus Christ, with all His power and perfection, made prayer a priority in His life, then where ought prayer to fit in your life and in mine?

ESPECIALLY THE BASICS

We depend upon God for everything, of course—for breath, for life, for companionship, for emotional support, for spiritual guidance, for vision, for hope. As Paul said to the philosophers in Athens, God gives to everyone "life, breath, and all things" (Acts 17:25).

And to help us remember all that, Jesus taught us to focus in prayer on our dependence on God for the daily supply of our material needs: "Give us this day our daily bread" (Matthew 6:11).

When Jesus told us to pray that, He especially had in mind the physical necessities of life represented by bread. The only reason we don't all die of starvation is that God is good and provides us with the food we need.

In Matthew 4:4, Jesus responded to one of the devil's temptations in the wilderness by quoting from Deuteronomy 8:3 and saying, "Man shall not live by bread alone, but by every word that proceeds from the mouth of God."

There's more to that verse than the simple truth that spiritual things are more important than material things. Bread itself would have no value to us unless its value had been supplied by the Creator.

Why is it that bread meets the needs of the human body? How is it that the plants which grow from the earth have the ability to supply us with strength? How can they help us to grow? It's possible only through the word that proceeds out of the

> *Were God to withdraw His word, bread would be useless to us.*

mouth of God. God speaks, and grain is given its nutritional properties. Were God to withdraw His word, bread would be useless to us; we might as well eat gravel.

It's the very word of God that sustains us. Hebrews 1:3 tells us that Christ is "upholding all things by the word of His power." And Paul told us that in Christ "all things hold together" (Colossians 1:17, NIV). There's nothing more basic to meeting our basic needs than the Word of God.

ON, IN, OVER

What are our basic needs? Essentially, we need something to put on us, something to put in us, and something to put over us. God says He'll take care of all three for us if we trust

Him. And as part of trusting Him, He wants us to ask Him for these things every day.

God wants us to ask for our daily bread not because He wants to hear us beg, but because He knows we have short memories and often forget that He's the One who supplies our every need. Praying daily for our bread helps fight our pride and materialism.

George Mueller knew all about asking for bread, and he saw God provide time after time in astonishing ways. I treasure the poem he crafted in response to God's faithfulness (as recorded in his biography by A. T. Pierson):

> I believe God answers prayer,
>   Answers always, everywhere;
> I may cast my anxious care,
>   Burdens I could never bear,
> On the God who heareth prayer.
>   Never need my soul despair
> Since He bids me boldly dare
>   To the secret place repair,
> There to prove He answers prayer.

Pointedly, Specifically

I talk with Christian people all the time who are in the midst of severe trials. Sometimes I ask them, "Have you ever asked God pointedly and specifically—naming the details of the situation—to help you and deliver you?" They often admit that they've prayed in general, though not specifically. But if you're in the lion's den, you need to pray about the lion; if you're in the fire, you need to pray about the flames.

Perhaps you're going through some particular struggles in your life right now, something very demanding and unsettling, and you wonder how God is going to take care of you.

If you're in the fire, you need to pray about the flames.

But if you aren't facing a trial at present, let me at least ask you this: What is it that you need now in your life more than anything else?

Name it.

Now…allow me to ask a pointed question. Have you asked God for this? Have you *really* asked Him?

And if you're undergoing a time of serious testing, have you asked God to provide exactly what you need to get through it? Have you prayed for Him to deliver you? Ask Him to do what He did for so many in the Bible. God still delivers! He's the same yesterday, today, and forever.

Maybe you need deliverance from fear. Sometimes, suddenly and out of nowhere, a spirit of fear grips my heart and I have to drop everything, leave my office, and go to a place I know by a lake. I talk and tell God about my fear, asking Him to deliver me from it.

Do you have any fears today? Have you asked God to take it away and to give you His peace and the strength that comes from knowing His presence?

You can say, "God, this situation is beyond me. I can't cope with it. But You can. Please extend Your hand, and help me and deliver me." Then tell Him all that you need.

There's no sickness that God cannot heal. There's no problem God cannot solve. There's no challenge God cannot meet. There's no financial deficit that God cannot overcome. There's no man who can overthrow God's purposes. There's no committee that can thwart God's work in the church of Jesus Christ.

So in prayer before His throne, make your declaration of dependence today…and every day.

Chapter 7

HOW TO PRAY

With such a God waiting to hear us, and such a privilege as prayer available to us for drawing close to Him and obtaining all His good gifts, why don't we do more asking?

The primary culprit is the enemy of our souls, who wants to keep us from developing a relationship that he knows will bring us joy and satisfaction. And I would hazard the guess that the enemy's number one strategy for preventing our prayer is simply the busyness of our lives. How often have you thought, *Oh, I really did mean to pray, but somehow I didn't get around to it.*

Jesus, too, was a busy man, yet He made time to pray. One particularly busy day for our Lord is recorded in Mark 1:21–34. It was a Sabbath, and Jesus was in the town of

Capernaum. He taught in their synagogue, astonishing His listeners with His authoritative teaching. A man was there who had an unclean spirit, and Jesus healed him, amazing the crowd even more. Then Jesus left the synagogue and went to the house of Simon and Andrew, where Simon's mother-in-law was bedridden with a fever. Jesus healed her, then she arose and served them.

After sunset, "the whole city" gathered at the door of the house, bringing "all who were sick and those who were demon-possessed." Jesus spent that entire evening healing and casting out demons.

Here was a day of the kind of intense, nonstop ministry that puts an unbelievable strain on both mind and body. After an exhausting day like that, most of us would want at least a full night's rest. But look at what Jesus did the next morning: "Having risen a long while before daylight, He went out and departed to a solitary place; and there He prayed" (Mark 1:35).

Oh, but that's Jesus, you may be thinking. He's the Son of God; of course He could do such a thing. I'm just an ordinary person, however. I could no more get up before dawn to pray on a morning like that than I could have healed all those people the night before. Jesus could do it; I can't.

We might like to follow our Master's example, but it

seems impossible. In fact, sometimes mere survival seems like the biggest success story we dare hope for. We feel we just don't have the strength to pray as Jesus did; it seems we're just too needy.

And yet that very thing is what most qualifies us to pray: our weakness, our neediness, our dependence, our helplessness.

The very thing that most qualifies us to pray is our helplessness.

"Prayer has been ordained only for the helpless," writes Ole Hallesby in his book *Prayer.* "Prayer and helplessness are inseparable. Only those who are helpless can truly pray." And Hallesby adds this: "Your helplessness is your best prayer."

That has to be the number one lesson in how to pray— simply let your helplessness be your guide.

Following is a summary of the other most important lessons I've learned.

PRAY PARTICULARLY

Jesus wants us to pray for specific things. He used bread and fish as illustrations in this text in Matthew 7—to teach His listeners about prayer, He used the common, ordinary needs of their lives.

When we pray, we're to pray particularly. Ask God what you want, specifically—specific enough so that when your request is answered, you'll know it, and praise and thank Him for it.

We must never make prayer into some spiritual make-believe game with no bearing on the actual needs that confront us. How often have we prayed something like this for others or for ourselves: "O Lord, be with them now in a special way"? But what are we really requesting? Imagine that you're a parent leaving your children with a new babysitter. Would you tell her, "Katie, I ask that you would be with my children now in a special way"? No, you would say, "The children need dinner, and then a bath and a Bible story before bedtime, and they're tired from a long day so make sure they're settled in bed by nine o'clock." You would be very specific with your requests. It should be the same in prayer.

> *Never make prayer into some spiritual make-believe game.*
>
> ❧

PRAY PERSONALLY

Some folks think prayer is almost exclusively a corporate activity. If they need prayer, they call the church and ask for everyone to be praying for them. That's a good thing to do, but corporate prayer is only as good as individual prayer.

Prayer is personal.

To ask as we should ask requires a regular measure of quietness before God, in solitude and separation. That's an issue I sometimes struggle with.

In Mark 1, after Jesus had risen long before dawn to go out alone and pray, His disciples went looking for Him. "Everyone is looking for You," they said when they found Him (Mark 1:37). I can relate to that to some degree; certainly not the whole world is looking for me, nor are they looking for me for the same reasons they looked for Jesus, but I feel the pressure, and I'm sure you sometimes do as well. And the principle we gain in this incident from Jesus' life is as valid for us as it was for Him: If Jesus, the Son of God, put into practice the discipline and determination to get away from the crowds so He could get alone with the Father to pray, so must we.

PRAY HONESTLY

In his introduction to the Psalms in *The Message* Eugene Peterson writes that because of our inexperience in prayer, "we suppose that there must be an 'insider' language that must be acquired before God takes us seriously in our prayer. There is not. Prayer is elemental, not advanced, language. It is the means by which our language becomes honest, true, and personal in response to God. It is the means by which we get everything in our lives out in the open before God."

God doesn't want us to shift into a stained-glass prayer voice.

God wants us to approach Him honestly, openly, and sincerely. Prayer is about real-world concerns, spoken in real-world language. God doesn't want us to shift into a stained-glass prayer voice to address Him.

When we read the Psalms, we see that David never tried to hide how he felt about things when he talked to God. He spoke plainly and honestly as he cried out to God. Sometimes we can hardly believe he's saying these things.

LEARN FROM OTHERS

During my long months of battling my illness, I not only prayed with greater urgency, but I also devoured the words of other saints who before me had begun their own adventures in prayer. I was encouraged and strengthened as I read their powerful insights. In my journal I copied the quotations that especially helped me.

That got me started in the practice of reading a chapter or short section from a book on prayer each day. I have to admit to you that I've practiced this for years in my own devotional life. Prayer is so hard for me that I'm always in the process of reading a book on prayer. I've probably read a hundred books on prayer. And I still struggle with prayer, but I know what to do.

Essentially you can learn to pray only by praying, but there are many books that can and will encourage you in this discipline.

PRAY PERSISTENTLY

Finally, remember to keep on asking, keep on seeking, and keep on knocking. Pray with persistence.

I learned many things from my professors in seminary. My all-time favorite was Howard Hendricks, the head of the department under which I studied. He's a tremendous communicator and a great man of God. One day he came into class, and with tears he announced, "Gentlemen, I want to tell you something. My seventy-year-old father received Jesus Christ as his Savior. That might not be meaningful to you until I also tell you that for forty years, I have prayed every day for his salvation. And after forty years, God finally said yes."

No wonder Jesus told us that we "should always pray and not give up."

It pays to pray. And it pays not to give up.

TWO STORIES

In Luke 11 and Luke 18, Jesus told His disciples two parables specifically to teach us not to be discouraged in our prayer lives. Obviously He considers losing heart in prayer to be a real possibility for us; just as obviously He considers prayer to be far too important for us to let it slide because of discouragement.

You may be discouraged in prayer right now—you keep trying to pray, but you can't be consistent with it. You may be discouraged because there's something you pray for every day, and still God hasn't answered your request. I, too, have fought discouragement in praying. I believe any honest Christian will confess to periods of discouragement in prayer, when it seems as if God were asleep or on vacation. That's why Jesus told these two stories.

A sense of acute need is the motivating factor in both these parables. Remember how the stories go?

In the first one (Luke 11:5–8), a man receives a visitor unexpectedly at his home. But it's late at night, and he has no food to refresh his guest after the long journey. So this determined host goes at midnight to knock at the door of his friend's house to ask for bread, even though the friend and all his family are asleep and their house shut tight. Will the host get the bread he seeks? Yes, Jesus says, he will—not because of any friendship, but simply because the man at the door is so persistent.

In the other parable (Luke 18:1–8), a widow keeps coming before a judge and asking him to grant her relief (probably financial relief) from an adversary. Will the widow get the justice she seeks? Yes, Jesus says, she will—not because of the judge's character and compassion (for this judge was "unjust" and "did not fear God nor regard man"), but simply because he's worn out by her persistent pleas.

And the lesson for us?

Jesus tells us: We "always ought to pray and not lose heart" (Luke 18:1), for God will most certainly "avenge His own elect who cry out day and night to Him," and He'll even do it "speedily" (Luke 18:7–8).

A main point in both these stories is *constancy* in prayer. Jesus was teaching us that no matter what we observe outwardly, no matter what seems to be coming back to us

By praying, we commit ourselves to Him.

through our sensory perceptions, the fundamental truth of our Christian life is wrapped up in our prayer to God. By praying, we commit ourselves to Him, and even though we can't see what He's doing, we know He's doing something and we won't abort that process by ceasing to pray. We won't lose hope; we won't get discouraged; we'll continue to pray.

PRAYER THAT WORKS

In Colossians 4:12, Paul tells the Colossians about his remarkable friend, Epaphras; he writes that Epaphras is "always laboring fervently for you in prayers." Another translation says that Epaphras was "always wrestling in prayer" (NIV). His prayer life had the intensity and all-out exertion of a wrestling match. He wrestled with God as Jacob did one night long before Paul's time (Genesis 32:22–32).

I wonder: Does that kind of language describe what our prayer life will be in the days ahead? Will it have the sheer intensity and exertion of an athletic contest? Will we be persistent? And will we make sure our prayer is particular, and personal, and honest?

To help you be able to answer yes to all those questions, there's one more practical thing I want to share with you about prayer.

Chapter 8

FOR THE RECORD

When I was a boy, my Uncle Clifford came to live with us for a while. Clifford was a quiet man who had faced a great many challenges in his life. But he was a godly saint, and years before he came to live with us, he'd begun keeping a diary. I can still remember him dragging out his seven-year journal after dinner and asking us if we knew what had happened on a particular date in any of the previous seven years. No doubt most of us kids yawned as we humored our uncle by listening to him read his short diary entries.

I remember thinking how strange it was that someone would take the time to write down what happened each day, and then refer to it later. What was the point?

That was my first encounter with journaling. As the years went by, my conviction solidified that macho men just didn't keep journals; journals were mostly for women and mystics, and I wasn't either.

SLOWING DOWN THE RPMS

Then my thinking started to change. A number of years ago I read something Bill Hybels wrote in *Too Busy Not to Pray,* about how journaling helped him bring more calmness and control to the start of his day:

> I have a high energy level in the morning. I can't wait to get to the office to start the day's work. And once the adrenaline starts flowing, the phone starts ringing, the people start coming, I can easily stay at ten thousand [RPMs] until I crash at night. So I decided to start journaling.... The amazing thing is what happens to my RPMs when I write. By the time I've finished a long paragraph recapping yesterday, my mind is off my responsibilities. I'm tuned in to what I'm doing and thinking, and my motor is slowed halfway down.

What Bill described about his life matched my own experience exactly. I often struggled with taking the time at the beginning of the day to focus on and listen to God. All I could think of was the huge list of to do's awaiting me. Could Bill be right about the power of journaling to slow one down at the beginning of the day?

In 1994, while recovering from cancer surgery, I received a copy of Gordon MacDonald's book *The Life God Blesses.* Since I was confined to a recliner for a few days, I started reading it…and couldn't put it down. As long as I could remember, I'd always wanted God to bless my life, and my bout with cancer had taken that desire to a whole new level.

In his book, Gordon described his personal discipline of journaling and mentioned that he did it on his computer. For some odd reason, that clicked with me. That very day I began to keep a record of God's dealings with me, using my computer.

Since then, I've been keeping a daily journal. I don't mean I never miss a day, but I've become committed enough to this discipline that whenever I do miss, I don't let it rob me of the joy of returning as soon as possible.

STAYING ON TRACK

More than anything else, this practice of journaling has reminded me that my walk with God is a daily experience that can be chronicled and measured. It not only helps me focus my prayer life, but is also an effective way to hold myself accountable to God's schedule for my life.

A journal is a diary, but it's much more than that. It's a daily account of spiritual progress in your walk with God, and it's especially valuable when it includes many of the prayers you ask and your record of how God has answered.

My walk with God can be chronicled and measured.

I must admit that when I first sat at the computer and started recording my prayers, if felt as if I were praying to my computer. But I soon got past that and began to realize the benefit of being precise in my conversation with the Lord. It was a great help for someone like me who has a difficult time staying on track while praying.

Once again, Bill Hybels gave me insight on this. "A good way to learn to pray specifically," he writes in *Too Busy Not to Pray,* "is to write out your prayers and then read them to God…. It forces me to be specific; broad generalities don't look good on paper. It keeps my mind from wandering. And it helps me see when God answers prayers."

MOMENTUM BUILDER

When we take the time (as I continue to learn to do) to write out some of our prayers, we discover areas of weakness that need to be strengthened and patterns of sin or foolishness that need to be corrected. We can also discover good patterns that are worth strengthening and encouraging.

When I've looked back at what I recorded in my journal, one thing I've observed is how consistently I sometimes ask God for something that I needed to take responsibility for myself. I was surprised how often I asked Him for the same thing. There was nothing wrong with my persistence in asking, but I could almost hear God saying to me as I read these entries, "David, why don't you just get control of your life and deal with these issues?"

I've been brought to tears on more than one occasion as I read my prayers in an early entry, then the record of God's answer in a later entry. God really heard me! He really did answer my prayer!

I've also recognized that I have a lot of growing to do in the art of intercession. I've made a good start, but I have a long way to go.

So as my last suggestion in this book, I encourage you to keep a journal—to help you respond to life honestly, to reflect on the meaning of your experiences, and to be specific in your requests to God.

You'll see the progress of your spiritual journey, which will help you regain momentum whenever you lose it. And more than anything else, you'll be encouraged to be faithful in prayer—to ask and keep on asking, to seek and keep on seeking, and to knock and keep on knocking.

Amen.

The publisher and author would love to hear your comments about this book. *Please contact us at:* www.bigchangemoments.com

OTHER LIFE-CHANGING TITLES
from *David Jeremiah*

PRAYER: THE GREAT ADVENTURE
Drawing from his personal prayer journals, David Jeremiah shares his heart—both his blessings and his struggles—to provide insights and teach readers how to embark on the great adventure of prayer.
ISBN 1-57673-486-2

THE POWER OF ENCOURAGEMENT
Encouragement breathes life into our souls. Without it, people die. *The Power of Encouragement* examines the heart of self-giving, genuine love and suggests helpful ways to learn to express the kind of encouragement that heals, unites, and renews people's zest for life.
ISBN 1-57673-135-9

GOD IN YOU
Life without the Holy Spirit is about as useful to God's kingdom as an unplugged toaster. Yet many people shy away from the Holy Spirit—usually because of unbalanced, unbiblical teaching. Let God release His power in you through the ministry of the Holy Spirit in the dynamic, life-changing book *God in You*.
ISBN 1-57673-717-9

WHAT THE BIBLE SAYS ABOUT ANGELS
Prominent Bible teacher David Jeremiah provides an in-depth, biblical look at the culturally hot topic of angels, correcting widespread misconceptions and giving a broad and thorough survey of scriptural teaching.
ISBN 1-57673-336-X

BIG CHANGE

TRUE FREEDOM
The Liberating Power of Prayer
OLIVER NORTH & BRIAN SMITH ISBN 1-59052-363-6

Honorary National Day of Prayer chairman Oliver North illustrates the freeing effects of prayer through engaging stories and scriptural truths.

THE PRAYER MATRIX
Plugging in to the Unseen Reality
DAVID JEREMIAH ISBN 1-59052-181-1
(Available February 2004)

Well-known radio minister David Jeremiah describes how God has ordained the processes of the world to work through the prayers of His people.

HOW GOOD IS GOOD ENOUGH?
ANDY STANLEY ISBN 1-59052-274-5

Find out why Jesus taught that goodness is not even a requirement to enter heaven—and why Christianity is beyond fair.

THE AIR I BREATHE
Worship as a Way of Life
LOUIE GIGLIO ISBN 1-59052-153-6

When we are awakened to the wonder of God's character and the cross of Christ, all of life becomes worship unto God.

SMALL BOOKS
BIG CHANGE

www.bigchangemoments.com

BIG CHANGE

GOD IS MORE THAN ENOUGH
TONY EVANS ISBN 1-59052-337-7

Dr. Tony Evans explains how your worries will melt away as you trust the Great Shepherd to meet your spiritual, directional, emotional, physical, and eternal needs.

THE FIRE THAT IGNITES
Living in the Power of the Holy Spirit
TONY EVANS ISBN 1-59052-083-1

Tony Evans reveals how the Holy Spirit can ignite a fire in your life today, transforming you from a sleepwalker into a wide-awake witness for Him!

WHAT'S SO SPIRITUAL ABOUT YOUR GIFTS?
HENRY BLACKABY ISBN 1-59052-344-X
(Available April 2004)

Find out from Henry Blackaby how spiritual gifts work for the common good of the body of Christ—and learn where you fit in.

WHAT THE SPIRIT IS SAYING TO THE CHURCHES
HENRY BLACKABY ISBN 1-59052-036-X

Learn how to listen to what the Holy Spirit is saying to you and to your church. Don't miss this release from Henry Blackaby, bestselling author of *Experiencing God*.
WHAT THE SPIRIT IS SAYING TO THE CHURCHES BIBLE STUDY
ISBN 1-59052-216-8

SMALL BOOKS
BIG CHANGE

www.bigchangemoments.com

BIG CHANGE

AFTER YOU'VE BLOWN IT
Reconnecting with God and Others
ERWIN LUTZER ISBN 1-59052-334-2
(Available March 2004)

Do you feel like God will never take you back? Would you like a
new beginning in your relationships? Award-winning author and
pastor Erwin Lutzer offers practical help toward reconciliation.

THE PURITY PRINCIPLE
God's Safeguards for Life's Dangerous Trails
RANDY ALCORN ISBN 1-59052-195-1

God has placed warning signs and guardrails to keep us from
plunging off the cliff. Find straight talk about sexual purity in
Randy Alcorn's one-stop handbook for you, your family, and
your church.

THE GRACE AND TRUTH PARADOX
Responding with Christlike Balance
RANDY ALCORN ISBN 1-59052-065-3

Living like Christ is a lot to ask! Discover Randy Alcorn's
two-point checklist for Christlikeness—and begin to measure
everything by the simple test of grace and truth.

A LITTLE POT OF OIL
A Life Overflowing
JILL BRISCOE ISBN 1-59052-234-6

What if He's asking you to pour out more than you can give?
Step into the forward motion of God's love—and find the
power of the Holy Spirit!

SMALL BOOKS
BIG CHANGE

www.bigchangemoments.com

BIG CHANGE

PRESSURE PROOF YOUR MARRIAGE
Family First Series, #3
DENNIS & BARBARA RAINEY ISBN 1-59052-211-7

Dennis and Barbara Rainey show you how to use pressure to your benefit, building intimacy with each other and with the Lord.

WRESTLING WITH GOD
Prayer That Never Gives Up
GREG LAURIE ISBN 1 59052 044 0

You struggle with God in your own unique way. See how your struggle can result in the most rewarding relationship with Him!

IN THE SECRET PLACE
For God and You Alone
J. OTIS LEDBETTER ISBN 1-59052-252-4

Receive answers to some of life's most perplexing questions—and find deeper fellowship alone in the place where God dwells.

OUR JEALOUS GOD
Love That Won't Let Me Go
BILL GOTHARD ISBN 1-59052-225-7

God's intense jealousy for you is your highest honor, an overflowing of sheer grace. And when you understand it better, it becomes a pathway to countless blessings.

SMALL BOOKS
BIG CHANGE

www.bigchangemoments.com

BIG CHANGE

GOD IS UP TO SOMETHING GREAT
Turning Your Yesterdays into Better Tomorrows
TONY EVANS ISBN 1-59052-038-6

THE HEART OF A TENDER WARRIOR
Becoming a Man of Purpose
STU WEBER ISBN 1-59052-039-4

SIMPLY JESUS
Experiencing the One Your Heart Longs For
JOSEPH M. STOWELL ISBN 1-57673-856-6

SIX STEPS TO SPIRITUAL REVIVAL
God's Awesome Power in Your Life
PAT ROBERTSON ISBN 1-59052-055-6

CERTAIN PEACE IN UNCERTAIN TIMES
Embracing Prayer in an Anxious Age
SHIRLEY DOBSON ISBN 1-57673-937-6

THE CROSS CENTERED LIFE
Experiencing the Power of the Gospel
C. J. MAHANEY ISBN 1-59052-045-9

THE DANGEROUS DUTY OF DELIGHT
The Glorified God and the Satisfied Soul
JOHN PIPER ISBN 1-57673-883-3

RIGHT WITH GOD
Loving Instruction from the Father's Heart
RON MEHL ISBN 1-59052-186-2

A PRAYER THAT MOVES HEAVEN
RON MEHL ISBN 1-57673-885-X

THE LOTUS AND THE CROSS
Jesus Talks with Buddha
RAVI ZACHARIAS ISBN 1-57673-854-X

SENSE AND SENSUALITY
Jesus Talks with Oscar Wilde
RAVI ZACHARIAS ISBN 1-59052-014-9

THE TREASURE PRINCIPLE
Discovering the Secret of Joyful Giving
RANDY ALCORN ISBN 1-57673-780-2
THE TREASURE PRINCIPLE BIBLE STUDY
ISBN 1-59052-187-0

GROWING A SPIRITUALLY STRONG FAMILY
Family First Series, #1
DENNIS & BARBARA RAINEY
ISBN 1-57673-778-0

TWO HEARTS PRAYING AS ONE
Family First Series, #2
DENNIS & BARBARA RAINEY
ISBN 1-59052-035-1

THE POWER OF CRYING OUT
When Prayer Becomes Mighty
BILL GOTHARD ISBN 1-59052-037-8

SMALL BOOKS
BIG CHANGE

www.bigchangemoments.com